DEPARTURE
GATE 2000

DEPARTURE GATE 2000

Classic Airliners 1975–1999

FREDDY BULLOCK

Airlife
England

First published in the UK in 2001
by Airlife Publishing Ltd

British Library Cataloguing-in-Publication Data
A catalogue record for this book
is available from the British Library

ISBN 1 84037 280 X

Typeset by Rowland Phototypesetting Limited, Bury St Edmunds, Suffolk
Printed in China

Airlife Publishing Ltd
101 Longden Road, Shrewsbury, SY3 9EB, England
E-mail: airlife@airlifebooks.com
Website: www.airlifebooks.com

Introduction

My interest in aviation began when I spent two enjoyable years between 1955 and 1957 performing my National Service duties, stationed for the most part at RAF Colerne situated on a hill above Bath Spa. During some of my off-duty periods I managed a series of flights, the first a trip in a Boulton-Paul Balliol, a two-seat single-engined trainer. I vividly remember doing a 'barrel roll' in this aircraft overhead Bristol. Other flights were in a Bristol Brigand two-engined aircraft followed by many trips onboard the Handley Page Hastings four-engined transport aircraft.

It was in 1975 that I began to photograph commercial aviation, and in this book I have put together approximately 140 slides highlighting airlines that are no longer in operation along with types and colour schemes that have disappeared from the aviation scene. During the last twenty-five years there have been many changes. While the older piston-engined aircraft have disappeared from the scene, they have been replaced with very efficient turbo-props used throughout the world mainly on short-haul commuter flights. The original classic jets are now being replaced in ever-increasing numbers by a new generation of cost-effective aircraft manufactured by Boeing and Airbus Industries, the two major builders left.

Aircraft photography can be very satisfying but also frustrating, especially at airports where the viewing facilities are poor. Fortunately there are airports around the world where good viewing areas exist. This is a hobby enjoyed by many, one that has given me immense pleasure over the years, I hope you will enjoy this book, a nostalgic look at the last twenty-five years of the twentieth century.

My thanks as always go to my wife Chris for her continuing support, and to everyone connected with the airline business, including my son Captain Simon Bullock and friend Captain Eon Michaelidies, both of British Midland. My younger son, Rupert, and my daughter, Sarah, are also thanked for their help.

Freddy Bullock
Huddersfield, England

McDonnell Douglas DC-4 LN-MOB of the Norwegian cargo operator Bergen Air Transport is seen arriving at Manchester airport in the late-afternoon light with a cargo charter, 19 March 1976.

Delta Air Transport, based in Brussels, were using this Convair 440 registered OO-VGJ on services to Amsterdam Schiphol from the Belgian capital in the mid-1970s. It is seen here at Schiphol.

Above: During 1977 Intra Airways of Jersey operated a series of regular weekend charters from Staverton near Gloucester using their fleet of DC-3s. G-AMYJ, painted in a new scheme, is ready for take-off for its flight to Jersey in the Channel Islands.

Right: In the late 1970s Miami was the place to view old piston-engined aircraft such as this Aesa DC-6B, YS-05C. Based in El Salvador, it was used purely for carrying cargo. This superb aircraft is seen parked at the cargo area in the Floridian city.

Above: With two engines feathered, Ilyushin 18 SP-LSB of the Polish airline LOT is seen taxiing to the gate at Manchester after a charter flight from Warsaw. It made a very pleasant sight on a lovely summer's evening in July 1976.

Right: Parked on the ramp at Miami, this Faucett of Peru DC-6B registered OB-R-750 looks in excellent condition despite its age.

Above: Andes Aerolineas Nacionales del Ecuador Canadair CL-44-6 HC-AYS shows off its classic design in the afternoon light on the ramp at Miami in April 1978.

Below: For many years the Vickers Viscount was the mainstay of the British Midland fleet before its replacement by the DC-9. G-BAPF, an 800 series, is taxiing for take-off from East Midlands airport on a flight to Amsterdam in September 1979.

Left: Formerly with British Airways, this Merchantman 953C, G-APES, was one of several purchased by Air Bridge Carriers for use by the company on their cargo services. It is seen at East Midlands airport in March 1979.

Below: Even by the late 1970s very few airlines used the de Havilland Heron on commercial services. One exception was Swift Aire, based in San Luis Obispo, California. N415SA sits outside the commuter terminal at Los Angeles International in March 1977.

With its smiling face, this Lockheed Electra, N6130A, was one of several used by PSA, complementing their fleet of Boeing 727s. It is seen at Los Angeles in March 1977.

Above: For a period Laker Airways flew one of their McDonnell Douglas DC-10-10s in the livery of Caribbean Airways for use on charters to that area. However, on 11 April 1977 G-BBSZ flew to Los Angeles, where it was photographed during its lay-over.

Left: Recently painted in the company's new scheme, Pakistan International DC-10-30 AP-AXC is ready to land at Heathrow. Delivered new to the airline on 1 March 1974, it was sold in 1986 and finally retired in October 1994.

Right: There's fog at London Heathrow in November 1975 and diversions are taking place, in this case to Manchester where we see Singapore Airlines Boeing 707-327C 9V-BDC side by side with TWA's Boeing 707-331B N8733. The latter aircraft was broken up at Davis-Monthan Airbase in Arizona during 1986.

Below: For a short period during the summer of 1978 Pan American leased this Northwest Orient Cargo Boeing 747-251F N616US, caught on camera at London Heathrow prior to departure from runway 27L. Delivered in July 1975, this aircraft has been with Northwest its entire life and is still in service.

Delivered new to American Airlines in
May 1971, this Boeing 747-123C was
sold to Trans Mediterranean Airways
in June 1976 and converted to cargo
configuration. OD-AGM is taxiing to
the cargo area at London Heathrow
after its flight from Beirut. Only in
service with TMA for eight months, it
was sold back to American Airlines
and eventually to UPS. It is still flying
as N675UP.

In 1978 this British Airways Concorde 102 G-BOAD was operated in dual BA and Singapore Airlines colours for services to Singapore, and is seen at Heathrow ready to take off from runway 27L.

Above: It's January 1978 and McDonnell Douglas DC-8-63CF HB-IDM of the Swiss charter company SATA, loaded with holidaymakers, proceeds to its take-off position at Las Palmas airport for a return flight to Zurich. It has since been converted to a DC-8-73CF and now flies with UPS as N810UP.

Left: Taxiing out from the gate at New York's John F. Kennedy airport, Allegheny's BAC 1-11-204AF N1124J is seen in the company's new colour scheme, which was beginning to appear when this picture was taken in April 1978. This aircraft was eventually scrapped in 1979 at Waco, Texas.

A familiar sight in the 1970s and 1980s was Dan-Air's Boeing 727s. On a September morning in 1979 this 100 series G-BAJW taxies from the terminal at East Midlands airport. It now flies in cargo mode with Northern Air Cargo of Anchorage, Alaska as N190AJ.

Left: Air California's Boeing 737-293 N462GB slows to a standstill at Orange County airport (now renamed John Wayne International) where the ground staff are ready for action. Note the freshly painted jeep. This aircraft was broken up in June 1994.

Below: Singapore Airlines Boeing 737-112 9V-BFF sits on the tarmac at Jakarta Halim International airport awaiting its return flight to Singapore. This aircraft later flew with Air Florida and the Mexican Air Force.

French-built Caravelles were very common in Europe during the 1970s. Sadly there are virtually none left flying today, but this picture of a JAT Caravelle, YU-AHG, arriving in Dusseldorf evokes some pleasant memories of these graceful-looking aircraft. This aircraft was withdrawn from service and broken up in October 1985.

With headquarters in Smyrna, Tennessee, Capitol International Airways flew charters and schedule services for many years before their eventual demise. McDonnell Douglas DC-8-63CF N907CL, wearing a new colour scheme, is about to land in Miami in March 1979. It presently flies with UPS as N867UP.

Above: Delivered new to Iraqi Airways in June 1976, this Boeing 747-270C was seized by Iran in 1991 during the war between the two countries and is presently stored out of use. In better times, on 18 August 1978, YI-AGN makes the final turn onto runway 27R at London Heathrow at the start of a flight to Baghdad.

Right: Built in 1961, this Air Rhodesia Boeing 720-025 was originally with Eastern Airlines of Miami before going into service in April 1973 with the Rhodesian airline. It is seen arriving at Jan Smuts Johannesburg airport after a flight from Salisbury (now Harare). The airline was eventually renamed Air Zimbabwe. The aircraft was put into storage in 1985 and was sold three years later, before finally being withdrawn in 1993.

Nicknamed 'Yellow Banana', Hughes
Airwest McDonnell Douglas DC-9-31
N9344 arrives at its stand at the
Mexican airport of Puerto Vallarta after
a flight from California. With its front
door opening, the automatic steps are
being extended. Photographed in
February 1976, it is still in service
with Northwest using the same
registration.

Right: In its early days Federal Express operated a large fleet of Dassault Falcon 20s for use on an ever-growing route network. This example, N8FE, sits in the afternoon sun at Los Angeles International awaiting its evening flight back to Memphis, Tennessee.

Below: Twelve days before its trade-in to Boeing I was lucky to catch Delta Air Lines Boeing 747-132 N9900 landing at Las Vegas after its flight from Atlanta. Later converted to cargo configuration and operated by Flying Tigers for a period, it now flies with Kitty Hawk International as N709CK.

Left: On a Sunday afternoon at London Heathrow in August 1976 VARIG Cargo's Boeing 707-341C PP-VJT turns onto the threshold of runway 09R at the start of its flight back to Brazil. Delivered in March 1967, this aircraft was damaged beyond repair at Manaus, Brazil, in June 1981.

Below: Only thirty-nine examples of the Convair 990 were ever built. The Spanish charter company Spantax became the largest operator of the type, which was frequently seen around Europe in the 1970s. EC-BZP is seen at Manchester in August 1979 after push-back, ready for its charter flight to Majorca.

One of the world's classic jets was the de Havilland Comet. After service with Kuwait Airlines and MEA, G-AYVS was purchased by Dan-Air in March 1971 and used by them until its withdrawal in January 1977. Sadly it was then broken up at the company's base in Lasham in April 1978. It is seen at Manchester in July 1976.

Above: Before the advent of the 'Jumbo' freighter, JAL Cargo extensively used the McDonnell Douglas DC-8-55F on worldwide cargo operations. JA8018 was photographed while unloading in Los Angeles in March 1977. It was bought by LAC Colombia in February 1995. It crashed near Asunción, Paraguay, in February 1996.

Below: In a new United Airlines scheme, a McDonnell Douglas DC-8-54F waits on the ramp at Los Angeles for its next load of cargo. N8049U was delivered to United in November 1966, and after several owners was purchased by Stage 3 Nacelle Inc. over thirty years later.

On a crisp late-September morning in 1979 Air Malta's Boeing 720-047B 9H-AAO is taxiing for take-off from East Midlands after an earlier diversion from Heathrow. Originally with Western Airlines of California, the aircraft spent eleven years with the Maltese airline. It was broken up in Arizona in 1990.

Used by Garuda Indonesian Airways for a period of fourteen years, McDonnell Douglas DC-8-55 PK-GEA sits on the ramp in Jakarta prior to a flight to Singapore in August 1974. Following service with LAC Colombia registered HK-3735X, the aircraft was withdrawn in 1993.

Above: South African Airways Boeing 727-44 ZS-SBG was purchased from the manufacturer in August 1967 and flew with the airline for fifteen years before being sold. It is seen arriving in Johannesburg in August 1975 after a flight from Durban. It was broken up at Opa Locka, Florida, in April 1998.

Below: Introduced in 1971, the Dassault Mercure was an unsuccessful attempt by the French manufacturer to enter the commercial market. Only ten aircraft were built, with Air Inter taking the balance. F-BTTI, in the company's new livery, prepares for take-off from Heathrow in September 1979. There are no Dassault Mercures in service today.

The Jordanian state airline Alia
purchased three Boeing 747-2D3Bs in
spring 1977. Used regularly on
services from Amman to Heathrow,
JY-AFB is seen on finals for landing on
runway 27L in August 1978. Sold and
converted to cargo configuration in
November 1991, it was eventually
operated by Atlas Air as N506MC.

In February 1978 two German charter companies merged to form Bavaria Germanair. Bearing the new titles, Airbus A300B4-2C D-AMAY is seen at Las Palmas.

Left: Iran Air's Boeing 707-386C EP-IRM catches the afternoon light at London Heathrow while turning onto runway 27R for take-off. Purchased new in March 1970, it is still in service with the company after twenty-nine years, but sadly no longer seen in London.

Below: New to Pan American in May 1966, this Boeing 727-21 was sold to Avianca Colombia as HK-1803 in November 1975. It was photographed while turning for take-off from Miami in April 1978. This aircraft was eventually destroyed when it crashed on a flight between Bogotá and Cali, Colombia, in November 1989.

One of the most beautiful aircraft ever to grace the skies was the Lockheed Constellation. In April 1981 I confess to being ecstatic when this 749A model belonging to Argo of the Dominican Republic landed in Miami. HI-328, with two engines feathered, was photographed while passing the author en route to its cargo area. Sadly, some months later it crashed into the sea short of the runway at Santo Domingo.

Left: Based at Denver's Stapleton airport, Comb's Aviation were a regional cargo carrier with a fleet of Convair 440 aircraft. N94CF sits on the ramp in the melting snow on Sunday 30 March 1980.

Below: Golden West were a small commuter airline based in Los Angeles, operating a small fleet comprising Twin Otters, Short 330s and two de Havilland Dash 7s, one of which, N702GW, waits on its stand at LAX in the company's new colour scheme. It was photographed in February 1981.

Above: This photograph of Falcon Airways ATL-98 Carvair N89FA, out of use at the time, was taken in February 1981 at Dallas Love Field airport. Based on a DC-4 airframe, these aircraft were developed by Aviation Traders Ltd of England for the carriage of vehicles across the English Channel. I vividly remember flying my own car in these interesting aircraft, which were powered by four 1,450 hp Pratt & Whitney piston engines. This aircraft is now with Academy Air of Griffin, Georgia.

Left: With engines running and passengers onboard, British Air Ferries Vickers Viscount 802 G-AOHM is ready for departure from Manchester airport on a domestic flight in June 1983.

Ransome Airlines de Havilland Dash 7
N176RA stands at its gate at New
York's La Guardia airport in September
1982. With a base in Philadelphia, the
company operated within the
Allegheny commuter partnership.

While passengers de-plane, the captain of this Air UK Handley Page Dart Herald 204 G-APWJ makes final adjustments to his documentation in June 1983 at Manchester.

Left: We're in Tucson, Arizona, in April 1982 where permission was granted to photograph this delightful Convair 440 N8042W of the local airline, Cochise. Note the vintage Chevron fuel truck behind.

Below: With its base in Killeen, Texas, Rio Airlines' aircraft were constant visitors to Dallas/Fort Worth International airport. Pictured here is Swearingen SA226TC Metro II N48RA with its engines running, ready to go.

Right: Having arrived in Memphis, Tennessee, from Chicago on a very wet Sunday in February 1982, a little time was spent on the ramp where I was lucky to catch this colourful de Havilland Riley Heron N714R of Semo Airways.

Below: Aspen Airlines, with their base at Denver Stapleton airport, Colorado, had a considerable fleet of Convair 580s which were painted in a variety of colours. With the snow-covered mountains for a backdrop, N5814 arrives at the small airfield of Lake Tahoe in April 1981.

Nearing the end of its long career, this classic Curtiss C-46 freighter of Rich International is seen on finals for landing in Miami, its home base. Sadly, N5370N no longer graces the skies.

Above: Recently taken over by Republic Airlines but still portraying the colours of previous owners North Central, with 'Herman the Duck' on its tail, Convair 580 N75170 and McDonnell Douglas DC-9-51 N765NC are both in push-back mode at Chicago O'Hare in April 1980.

Left: On a bright and breezy day this scene at Sumburgh in the Shetland Islands shows British Vickers Viscount 804 G-CSZB parked on the ramp after its flight from Aberdeen. These flights were on contract to ferry oil rig workers to the island for a final helicopter trip out to the rigs in the North Sea. My eldest son, Simon, was First Officer on the flight, and I was fortunate to be in the jump seat for both flights.

Left: With rain clouds threatening, British Caledonian McDonnell Douglas DC-10-30 G-BGAT is ready to depart from London Gatwick on a schedule flight to South America in August 1980. This aircraft is presently with Continental Airlines, registered N13066.

Below: Flying Tigers Boeing 747-245F N815FT was a mere four months old when photographed arriving at Los Angeles International in February 1981. It presently flies with Cargo Air Lines as 4X-AXK.

Above: Before Miami-based National Airlines' takeover by Pan Am, Boeing 727-51 N5608 was photographed at New York's La Guardia airport in March 1980 at the start of a flight to its home base in Florida. The aircraft was broken up in May 1994.

Right: Owned by the Texas Air Corporation, New York Air were based at the city's La Guardia airport, the scene of McDonnell Douglas DC-9-31 N1311T turning into its gate. Eventually absorbed into Continental Airlines and re-registered N14564, it has now been withdrawn from service.

Above: World Airways McDonnell Douglas DC-10-30CF N108WA was one of twelve purchased new from 1979 onwards for charter and leasing contracts in which the company specialised. It is seen parked at Los Angeles in February 1982. It now flies with FedEx as N318FE.

Left: In the warmth of the Canary Islands, Scanair's McDonnell Douglas DC-8-55 LN-MOH is next to depart from Las Palmas, taking holidaymakers home to the cold of Oslo, Norway. Today, after thirty-three years in service, it flies with Kitty Hawk International as N807CK.

Boeing 737-2T5 G-BGTW was built new for Orion, based at East Midlands airport, in February 1980. G-BGTW taxies to its take-off position on a charter flight from Manchester in May 1981. With the company no longer in business, the aircraft is now with Ryanair, registered EI-CKS.

Airbus A300B4-203 OH-LAA was one of two originally bought by Finnair but subsequently transferred to Kar Air for use by the charter company. A regular visitor to the island of Gran Canaria, this aircraft, photographed in January 1988, will shortly depart from Las Palmas on a flight back to Helsinki. The aircraft is now operated by Air Scandic as G-TTMC.

Delivered to BOAC as G-ARVJ in May 1964, this VC10-1101 was leased to the Qatar Government in October 1975 and flown in the colours of Gulf Air. It was seen arriving at its stand within Terminal 2 at London Heathrow in May 1981 with a VIP flight. G-ARVJ is presently in service with the Royal Air Force.

Left: Originally operated by Alitalia Cargo, McDonnell Douglas DC-9-32F N935F was purchased by Evergreen International in October 1981. It was photographed in Los Angeles in February 1982 in its new paint scheme. The aircraft was sold to USA Jet Airlines in 2000 as N208US.

Below: Once a familiar sight, Trident 3 G-AWZL is shown at Manchester's domestic terminal in September 1980 preparing to depart on a 'shuttle' flight to Heathrow. The 'British' title was used only for a short period.

Above: Boeing 747-127 N601BN was bought by Braniff International in January 1971 and was soon given the nickname 'Big Orange'. For many years this aircraft plied its trade between Dallas/Fort Worth and Honolulu. When the company expanded into Europe it occasionally visited London Gatwick. Sadly, the company went out of business and the aircraft was then used by Tower Air for ten years before it was scrapped in May 1994. N601BN is seen here at Dallas in February 1981.

Below: Dutch charter company Martinair used the Airbus A310 for some years before selling its fleet to Federal Express for cargo conversion. In January 1988 A310-203 PH-MCA was photographed in Las Palmas taxiing for its return to Amsterdam.

Above: 9G-ABO, a VC10-1102 of Ghana Airways, begins to roll down runway 09R at London Heathrow in November 1980. Purchased new in January 1965 it spent its entire career with the airline before withdrawal and storage at Prestwick in December 1980. It was broken up in 1983.

Left: Before the demolition of the Berlin Wall and the reunification of Germany, all flights from the city were flown by Western-based companies. American-owned Air Berlin operated charter flights. Boeing 707-331 N767AB was the next aircraft to depart from Las Palmas on its flight to Berlin's Tegel airport when it was photographed in January 1980. It was broken up at Stansted in May 1981.

Still bearing its American registration N762TW, this former TWA Boeing 707-331 was leased to Air Tanzania for a period in the early 1980s. Used on services from Dar-es-Salaam, it was photographed at London Gatwick in August 1980.

Above: Purchased from Eastern Airlines in April 1981, Aces Colombia Boeing 727-25 HK-2604X sits on the ramp gleaming in its new paint while awaiting delivery. The aircraft is now operated by FedEx as N154FE.

Left: Airbus A300B4-203 C-GIZJ was one of three leased by Canadian charter company Wardair from South African Airways in the early 1980s. It was photographed at Fort Lauderdale while taxiing for take-off on a flight to Vancouver in February 1989. The aircraft is now registered ZS-SDE and back in service with South African Airways.

Delivered new to Korean Airlines in May 1981, Boeing 747-2B5F HL7459 was leased immediately to Saudi Arabian Airlines. A pure cargo aircraft, it has just landed at London Heathrow (3 September 1981) and is taxiing to the cargo area on the south side of the airfield. It is still in service with Korean.

Above: Formerly with Pan American, Boeing 707-321B N402PA spent just over a year in the service of charter company American Eagle based in Baltimore, Maryland. The aircraft is seen at Las Vegas in April 1981. It was eventually broken up at Davis-Monthan Airbase.

Left: In the early 1980s Alia Royal Jordanian painted several of their Lockheed TriStar 500s in various schemes for evaluation. We see JY-AGA at Heathrow in a scheme that was not adopted, on 7 October 1981.

When National Airlines were taken over by Pan American their entire fleet was repainted, an example being this McDonnell Douglas DC-10-10, N67NA, seen ready for take-off from Miami. Sold and later used by American Airlines, the aircraft was retired in 1995.

Delivered new to Transamerica in
December 1979, N741TV was one of
three Boeing 747-271Cs bought by the
company for their charter operations.
A frequent visitor to Manchester, this
aircraft is taxiing away from its gate
preparing for a flight to Los Angeles. It
is now registered N538MC and owned
by Atlas Air.

Left: This McDonnell Douglas DC-8-33F was originally bought new by Pan American in November 1960. After spending a few years with Rich International of Miami as N8166A, it was later sold and finally scrapped in Luanda, Angola, in May 1988.

Below: Originally purchased in 1968 by Airlift International, this colourful Boeing 727-172C, N727AL, was owned by Miami-based Southeast for less than a year. Photographed in January 1982, the aircraft has had many owners since that date. It is presently owned by Kelowna Flightcraft Air Charter of Edmonton, Alberta, and flown in the colours of Purolator Courier, registered C-GKFT.

With snow on the ground at Denver
Stapleton airport and in freezing
temperatures, Frontier's Boeing 737s
make an interesting line-up in March
1980.

Above: For a short period British Airways decided to be known simply as 'British'. An example of this is the company Boeing 707-436, G-AXXY, in position for take-off from runway 27L at London Heathrow in August 1980. It was broken up for spares at Tucson, Arizona, in the late 1980s.

Below: Braniff International, based in Dallas, Texas, were renowned for the diverse colour schemes on their aircraft. This picture captures the only Boeing 747SP-27, N606BN, ever to be operated by the company, about to land at Miami in January 1982. The aircraft flies today as A40-SP with the Oman Royal Flight.

Above: Air Florida's Boeing 737-222, an ex-United aircraft registered N69AF, taxies to the gate at Dallas/Fort Worth International after a flight from Miami in February 1981. The aircraft is now registered XA-SYX and flies with Magnicharters of Mexico.

Below: With storm clouds looming in the background, Tampa Colombia's Boeing 707-324C, HK2600X, is busy unloading its cargo in Miami in April 1981, still wearing British Caledonian's cheatline. This aircraft was damaged beyond repair in an accident at São Paulo, Brazil, in October 1994.

Above: Having flown from Las Vegas on this former Hughes Airwest Boeing 727-2M7, N727RW, I duly photographed it on the ramp at Tucson on 6 April 1981. After its time with Republic, the aircraft went to Northwest, who still use it.

Below: McDonnell Douglas DC-10-10 N902WA was purchased new by Western Airlines in June 1973 and remained in service with the airline for fourteen years. It is seen about to take off from Miami in the late afternoon in April 1981, its destination Los Angeles. With the company's take-over by Delta, the aircraft was sold.

Bought in August 1961 by Eastern
Airlines, McDonnell Douglas
DC-8-21, N1976P, saw many owners
before it was retired in July 1992.
Owned by Texas Air Carriers for two
years (1981 and 1982), it was still
wearing this splendid scheme
celebrating the USA's bicentenary
when photographed in February 1982,
parked in the cargo area of Dallas/Fort
Worth International.

Japan Airlines purchased this McDonnell Douglas DC-8-33 in May 1961; it was sold to American Jet Industries and registered N124AJ in 1975. Converted into a freighter, it was used by many companies prior to being broken up in August 1985. It is seen at Miami painted in the colours of Central American Air Cargo in January 1982.

The early-morning mist is clearing at Manchester airport in August 1981 as HB-ISL readies itself for Swissair's flight to Zurich. At this time the flights were operated by McDonnell Douglas DC-9-51s. HB-ISL was sold in 1987 to Scandinavian Airlines. Its present whereabouts are unknown.

Less than a year in service and wearing the company's old scheme, Korean Air Lines Boeing 747SP-35 HL7457 arrives in Los Angeles in February 1982 after its flight across the Pacific from Seoul. It is one of two 747SPs operated by the airline, both of which were withdrawn at the end of 1998 after spending their entire lives with Korean. Both are currently stored at Marana, Arizona.

One of Braniff Airways' many schemes
is seen on McDonnell Douglas DC-8-62
N1805, which catches the evening
light as it turns for take-off on runway
12 at Miami in April 1981. Delivered
new to the airline in September 1967,
it eventually went to Rich
International in 1983 before being
retired in 1990.

Above: Delivered new to Viasa in September 1961 as YV-C-VIB, this Convair 880 flew with the airline for seven years before moving on to several owners. For a short period in 1981, and re-registered N48063, it was used by Sunjet International, and is seen at Miami in April of that year. It was broken up in 1984.

Below: Built in 1968, N15711, a Boeing 707-331C, spent most of its working life with TWA until it was leased to Air Haiti for nearly two years. Used in cargo mode, it is seen in Miami in April 1980. It was broken up for spares at Davis-Monthan AFB, Tucson, in the mid-1980s.

Used by American Airlines and Pan American from 1961 to 1971, this Boeing 720-023B was eventually bought by Ecuatoriana as HC-AZQ and operated by them for eleven years. Repainted in this superb scheme, it prepares for take-off from Miami bound for Quito in April 1981. It was broken up in Tucson in 1985.

Originally ordered by Braniff but not taken up, this Boeing 727-227 was leased by Air Florida as N274AF and used for only one year before being repossessed. It presently flies with American Trans Air as N779AT.

Above: Another McDonnell Douglas DC-8-62 operated by Braniff Airways (see page 68), N1803 is also seen in Miami in April 1981, this time in a dark green colour scheme. Converted to cargo configuration in July 1985, it was used by Cargosur and Arrow Air before retirement in the 1990s.

Left: Built in 1975 and delivered to the Dutch charter company Transavia as PH-TVE, this Boeing 737-2K2C was leased by Air Malta for a period of two years commencing in October 1980. The cargo door is clearly visible as the aircraft taxies for take-off from Manchester in August 1981. The aircraft is still in service with Aeropostale as F-GGVQ.

Right: Another new American airline which did not survive for long was Jet Train. Seen landing at Fort Lauderdale in January 1996 is McDonnell Douglas DC-9-31 N8927E, a former Eastern Airlines aircraft. Operations were suspended in November that year. The aircraft is now operated by Ascerca of Venezuela registered YV-708C.

Below: Seen at Palm Springs in April 1996 is new start-up airline Air 21's Fokker F-28-4000, N498US, one of three leased from USAir to operate their services. Like so many new airlines they lasted only a short while. The aircraft is stored at Marana, Arizona.

Air Hong Kong's Boeing 747-132SCD
VR-HKN is seen on final approach to
runway 06 at Manchester airport in
May 1995 after a schedule cargo flight
from Hong Kong. It was retired and
sold to Polar Air Cargo in July 1996 as
N856FT. The aircraft is now stored at
Marana, Arizona.

In January 1996 the German commuter airline Interot was renamed Augsburg Airways. Wearing both titles for a short period, de Havilland Dash 8-103A D-BAGB was photographed while proceeding to its stand at Dusseldorf later that year.

There is no doubting which country this Boeing 737-3M8 HB-IIA comes from. With the terminal in the background, HB-IIA is seen turning towards runway 03 for take-off from Lanzarote for TEA Switzerland's flight back to Zurich. The company was taken over by Easy Jet in 1999 and the aircraft have been repainted.

Right: Formed in 1988, Carnival Air Lines ceased to exist in mid-1996 when the company was bought by the resurrected Pan Am. On 30 December 1995 Boeing 737-4Q8 N405KW taxies for departure at Fort Lauderdale. The aircraft presently flies with Olympic Airways as SX-BKI.

Below: Sunways' aircraft were regular visitors to Manchester on charters from Turkey between 1995 and 1997. The airline ceased operations at the end of 1997. Sunways had aircraft registered in Sweden and Turkey; this picture shows Boeing 757-23C SE-DSL and McDonnell Douglas DC-9-83 TC-INC in August 1996.

While Deutsche BA is still very much
in business, they no longer use the
Fokker 100. In old colours, D-ADFD is
seen at Dusseldorf in September 1996.
The aircraft is now owned by Air
Liberté, registered as F-GNLJ.

Right: To promote the 1996 Olympic Games held in Atlanta, Delta Air Lines painted Boeing 767-232 N102DA in a special scheme. It is seen ready for departure from Fort Lauderdale in January of that year. An MD-11 was similarly treated. Both have since been repainted.

Below: New to TWA in April 1969 and in service with the airline for twenty years, Boeing 727-231 N74318 has since been used by several start-up airlines, including Sunair. The aircraft is seen landing at Fort Lauderdale in 1996.

In May 1991 VARIG leased this Boeing 747-475, PP-VPI, to provide additional capacity on their international routes. With a downturn in the Brazilian economy it was returned in August 1994 and now flies with Air New Zealand as ZK-SUH.

It seemed appropriate to include what is known to enthusiasts as a 'white tail'. In good light, McDonnell Douglas DC-8-62F OB-1618 of Peruvian carrier Faucett, wearing just cargo titles, prepares to land in Miami in January 1996.

Translift Airbus A320-231 EI-TLJ about to touch down in Miami while on a winter lease to Trans Meridian of Houston, Texas.

Left: Leased for the winter season of 1995/96 by Carnival Air Lines of Fort Lauderdale, Pegasus Boeing 737-4Q8 TC-AFM prepares to land at Miami in January 1996.

Below: Air Namibia's sole Boeing 737-25A, V5-ANA, sits at the gate in Cape Town before its return to Windhoek. This aircraft was new to Midway Airlines in August 1987 and was then purchased by Namib Air in May 1991. The airline was renamed Air Namibia in October 1991.

With a fleet of seven Boeing 737-200s, Air South commenced operations from their base in Colombia, South Carolina, in 1994, but sadly went out of business in 1997. EL-CKL is landing in Miami in December 1995. The aircraft currently flies with Aerolineas Argentinas as LV-YIB.

Purchased by TWA in May 1971, this classic Boeing 747-131, N93117, spent most of its working life with the company before retirement in 1992. The aircraft is seen in the colours of Family Airlines (a start-up failure) while in storage at Mojave in April 1996. It was eventually broken up here in October 1998. Note the British Airways TriStars in the background.

A delightful line-up at New York's La Guardia airport in March 1980: a National DC-10, a United B727, an Ozark DC-9 and a Republic DC-9

Above: Air Holland's Boeing 757-2T7 PH-AHO looks striking as it turns for take-off from the island of Lanzarote in January 1998 on a return charter to Rotterdam. The company ceased operations in November 1999.

Below: Of the two BAe 146-200s used by the Isle of Man regional airline Manx, one aircraft was painted in company colours. G-MIMA is seen arriving in Dusseldorf with the morning flight from Manchester. It currently wears a special Manx scheme.

In pouring rain Crossair's McDonnell Douglas DC-9-83 HB-IUH with its distinctive McDonald's livery is in the process of push-back from its gate at the start of a charter flight from Zurich in June 1999. This aircraft has now been repainted in a new scheme.

Above: A busy scene at Flughafen Frankfurt-Main as Continental's Boeing 747-238B N607PE is pushed from the gate at the start of a transatlantic flight. Formerly a Qantas aircraft, later owned by People Express, it was absorbed into Continental when they purchased the latter airline and is now owned by Tower Air under the registration N607FF.

Right: Taken over by the British tour operator Britannia in 1997, Blue Scandinavia's Boeing 757-2Y0, SE-DUL, still wears its original colours in January 1998. It is about to depart from Lanzarote on a return flight to Malmö, Sweden. The aircraft has since been repainted in Britannia's colour scheme.

When USAir purchased PSA they took
onboard their fleet of BAe 146-200s
and repainted them in house colours,
as illustrated in this picture of
N183US taken in Los Angeles in
October 1990. They were all withdrawn
from service soon after and placed in
storage at Mojave. I remember
seeing them lined up there in 1994.

Bought by American Airlines in December 1966, this Boeing 727-23F was converted to freighter configuration in 1985 by Flying Tiger Line and was subsequently leased in November 1991 by AECA Aeroservicios Ecuatorianos. The aircraft is now with SMA Cargo Airlines of Nigeria as 5N-SMA. It is seen landing at Miami in February 1992.

The newly-formed Euroscot leased this BAC 111-510ED from European Aviation to provide services. Painted in Euroscot's own colours, G-AVMT arrives in Dusseldorf on a proving flight in September 1997. The airline's operations ceased in July 1999.

Right: Sitting side by side at East Midlands airport in August 1992 these two British Midland McDonnell Douglas DC-9-15s G-BMAB and G-BMAA rest between flights, the latter flying the service to Frankfurt. Both these aircraft are now with Intercontinental de Aviacion of Bogotá, registered HK-3958X and HK-3827X.

Below: Long gone from the aviation scene are the Dassault Falcon 20s used by Purolator Courier. In happier times N300JJ sits the day out at Los Angeles International airport before its regular night-time flight.

Above: In October 1990 Hawaiian Air McDonnell Douglas DC-8-62 N8970U, formerly with United Airlines, sits at the gate in Honolulu for the once-weekly flight to Papeete and Rarotonga in the Cook Islands. Despite flying around Rarotonga for fifty minutes because of hydraulic problems prior to landing, I remember my flight on this as one of the best I ever had on a classic jet. The aircraft is now used as a corporate jet by the Australian Consolidated Press and registered VP-BLG.

Right: Canadian Pacific McDonnell Douglas DC-8-63 C-FCPS, wearing Skybus/Aérobus titles, has just been pushed back from the gate at Manchester airport in September 1980 at the start of a charter flight to Toronto. It crashed on take-off from Kansas City airport, Missouri, in February 1995 while being used by Air Transport International.

This former Pan American Boeing 707-321C was used in cargo mode by Türk Hava Yollari (Turkish Airlines). Registered TC-JCC, it is seen at London Heathrow in September 1981. After nine years in service with the airline it was sold. Leased by Golden Star Air Cargo in January 1991 as ST-ALX, it crashed into Mount Hymittus, Greece, twelve months later.

In the days before Terminal 2 was built at Manchester airport, viewing was excellent from the spectators' terrace. In May 1979 I had this superb view of Ontario Worldair Boeing 707-338C C-GRYN arriving on a charter flight from Toronto. Originally with Qantas, this aircraft eventually finished its career with the Royal Australian Air Force.

Frequent visitors to Manchester on charters from Vancouver were Wardair's Boeing 747s and McDonnell Douglas DC-10-30s. An example of the latter, C-GXRB, is seen arriving mid-morning. The aircraft currently flies with DAS Air Cargo, registered N100JR.

Guernsey Airlines' sole Viscount 735,
G-BFYZ, sits on the tarmac at
Manchester airport in between flights
in May 1979.

In the summer of 1981 Air Florida leased this McDonnell Douglas DC-10-30CF, N1035F, from Overseas National. It is seen after arriving in Manchester on a flight from Orlando in April 1981. The aircraft currently flies with FedEx as N304FE.

Another former Pan Am Boeing 707-321C, HC-BGP spent some time in service with Ecuatoriana Jet Cargo, flying principally from the Ecuadorian capital, Quito, to Miami. It was photographed while lined up for take-off from the latter city in February 1992. The aircraft is currently in service with AECA (Aeroservicios Ecuatorianos).

Boeing 707-436 G-APFD was purchased new in April 1960 by British Overseas
Airways Corporation (BOAC). Transferred to the British Airtours division in
April 1974, it was then leased to Air Mauritius for a period before returning. This
resulted in the hybrid scheme seen on the aircraft at Manchester in July 1979. It
was broken up in Fort Lauderdale in August 1986.

Laker Airways Airbus A300B4-203 G-BIMB was a mere six months old when I photographed it at Manchester in August 1981. With the demise of the airline in February 1982 it was placed in storage at Stansted airport before its lease to Air Jamaica as 6Y-JMK a year later. The aircraft is now in service with TransAer as EI-TLQ.

A former Eastern Airlines Boeing 727-25 (N8140N), this aircraft was purchased by Trump Shuttle in June 1989 and re-registered N904TS. This company in turn was taken over by USAir Shuttle with the new title being applied just two months after this picture was taken, in Miami in Febuary 1992. It was purchased as 9Q-CWT in July 1994 by Wetrafa Airlift of Kinshasa, where it is now stored.

Above: With a new paint scheme and new titles Air Cal (formerly Air California), McDonnell Douglas DC-9-82 N479AC is ready for push-back at the then Orange County airport in February 1982. With the demise of the airline this aircraft eventually went to Continental, with whom it still flies today.

Left: TWA took delivery of this Boeing 707-331C in October 1967. After eleven years it was sold to Fast Air of Chile as CC-CAF, who then sold it to Aerolineas Uruguayas Cargo in March 1990. Under the ownership of First International Airlines as P4-OOO, it was destroyed while landing at Kinshasa, Zaire, in January 1997.

Boeing 727-225 N8855E sits forlornly in the desert at Mojave, California, in March 1994 in the colours of Braniff International after the third attempt to resurrect this famous airline failed. Following further service with various airlines it was broken up in Miami in 1998.

Used from new in 1980, Boeing 727-290, N295AS, spent ten years flying with Alaska Airways before it was sold. Since then it has flown with various small start-up companies, one of which was Fort Lauderdale-based Av Atlantic. The aircraft is seen here on approach to Miami International airport in early 1996. With the airline no longer in business the aircraft is now owned by Champion Air of Bloomington, Indiana.

Above: This ex-Eastern Airlines aircraft, a McDonnell Douglas DC-9-31, N8925E, resides in the Mojave desert awaiting new owners. Only in service with Midway Airlines for five months prior to storage it was later sold to Northwest, who operate the aircraft to this date.

Left: KLM purchased this McDonnell Douglas DC-9-32 in 1968 and used it for nearly twenty years before it was bought by Midway Airlines as N946ML. Following various periods of storage it was eventually purchased by ValuJet of Atlanta. It is seen at Fort Lauderdale in January 1996 prior to being re-registered N967VV. Following a tragic accident the company ceased flying and was then relaunched as Air Tran Airways. The aircraft is now registered N867AT.

Index of Aircraft Types